STAY (Don't You Want To See How It Ends?)

Jenna Brandt

Presentation by *BookLeaf Publishing*

Web: www.bookleafpub.com

E-mail: info@bookleafpub.com

ISBN: 9789358736557

First edition 2023

*To anyone who has ever felt like they could not
make it through one more day…please just
STAY*

www.thetrevorproject.org has great resources

To Margie, Sherrie and Candace

*Thank You for always being there to help
process my thoughts and feelings and always
wanting to hear my poetry.*

To Stella and Stevie

I love you both, always.

No Matter What!

Always and Forever

ACKNOWLEDGEMENT

The following artists and authors The Tragically Hip, R.E.M, Florence and The Machine and Lewis Carroll.

PREFACE

"I wish I knew how this would all turn out" said the rabbit

"Maybe it's not about knowing how it will turn out" said the ox

"Maybe what you really want to know is that you'll be ok no matter what happens"

The Oxherd Boy

Dear Depression

Why do you always come for me?
I have got rid of you before
But you keep coming back to me.
I am weak.
This time you may win this battle
But I wont give up.
I promise u this
I will not go down without a fight.
Depression you hurt me.
You make people not know me,
You make me not know me,
You make me cry.
You make me bleed.
Dear depression
Let me be.

Loose Girl

Maybe I'm just destined to be a loose girl.
I am hard to love, though easy to please
I believe words and look over actions
Maybe I will always be a loose girl.
I am too deep, too dark, to be loved
My body may not be pretty but I have a body
a body one can take, use and abuse
A mind easy manipulated but that just wants
affection and love
Maybe I will always be a loose girl.
Maybe that's all I'm worth.
Love is over rated and never real when your just
worth enough to be a loose girl.
I wanna make you happy so I'll give you what
you want
in hopes you'll love me how I want
I will always be a loose girl.
How can I not be a loose girl?
That's all I'm good for
is a loose girl.

The Last Night

Some may say suicide is the most selfish thing
one could do
Instead of one ending the pain they feel,
it just passes it on to someone new
Someone who could never understand how one
could take there own life,
they've never even thought of picking up a
kitchen knife
They've had their bad days like everyone does,
but they've still never thought,
this is it
I've had enough.
But if you've never lived a life that makes you
question why,
why
Am I
still here,
I just want to die.
Sometimes being selfish is what one has to be,
sometimes six feet under
feels more free.
I may choose to be selfish that's my choice to do.
It doesn't mean I didn't love you or I didn't want
to try

I just believe one should control when they say
goodbye.
My pain ends with me,
you don't have to take it on,
your story is your story
and hey,
life
goes
on.

Remember the life that I lived. Not how I died.

It's Time

Life wasn't beautiful to her like it seemed to be
for everyone else,
No matter how many times she was told she had
a purpose,
She could never just figure hers out.
She had lots to be thankful for although life had
not always been kind,
But still she could never get the thought out of
her mind.
She had many dreams but only one she wanted
most,
To feel the way others feel or
Take the selfish way out.
One on the outside could never understand how
this could girl spend her days wondering
When it will end, not for everyone else
Just for the voices in her head.
The voices telling her life just doesn't make
sense,
You will feel much more at peace being six feet
under instead.
Life is too short they say
Not for her
It was too long,
All she needed to do was hear just

One more song,
One song to try and change mind,
One song to make her see, that life was beautiful
But she had already made up her mind
She had written
                        the letter,
She had made
                        the call,
She put her favourite song on repeat - drowning
out it all.
It was time to go,
It was time for the confusion to end,
Although she would leave the ones behind her in
pain,
She was selfish and now maybe they will feel
the same.
The same way she had felt
As long as she can remember,
That life is not beautiful
Its heartache and pain and only the ones who are
meant to be here will be Unchanged…

Do You Ever Wonder?

Do you ever wonder what happened to me?
Cuz I wonder what ever happened to you
Remember when everything was brand new
Everything felt fun, we could do no wrong

Do you ever wonder if we did not meet?
Would our lives be the same, or would it have
skipped a beat

Do you every wonder if we did not fall in love?
We could of kept dreaming for the high sky
above

Do you ever wonder why you let me walk away
that night?
Even though it was just another silly fight

Do you ever wonder if I do get my wish?
To live high in the sky and the wind will be my
kiss

Do you every wonder if life is all just a dream?
Wake up, your hearts racing, you want to
scream..

Do you ever wonder what happened to me?
Because I wonder what happened to you

STAY

It's been a year but not much has become clearer
I still think about it everyday
I think about still what someone could say to
make me really, truly want to stay
I have done a lot of work and healing but I still
can't find life's meaning
I don't understand why we are all alive and work
so hard to strive and survive
In the end it's all the same, si xfeet under or
ashes to spread while saying your name
Believe me I'm trying - I'm trying everyday
I continue to fight no matter what I say
I want these thoughts to leave my Brain
I wonder what it's like to feel sane
Each day I wake up and sometimes wonder why
I usually let out a quiet sigh
I want to be happy I want to find purpose
Have all things really come to the surface?
I have so many blessings each and everyday,
mind,
please change how you think and want to stay
I'll keep fighting my body and mind are tired but
the universe, I guess, told me my life is not yet
expired

I am sorry everyday for all the pain I made my
loved ones feel
I am going to make you a deal
I promise I will keep fighting each and everyday,
I will be honest with what I say
There are many moments I reflect on each day
and they are becoming
more and more reasons
to
stay

I'm Lying

Im sorry I'm lying
I really don't feel like trying
I don't want to "join the fight"
I just want it to end tonight
It's all I think about, all I dream
All I want to do is scream
Please let me die, and finally be able to fly high
It's always hard to say goodbye
I'm sorry I'm going to make you cry
I gave it another year, 365 days, sometimes it all
feels like a haze
I have had lots of blessings and days that make
me want to "join the fight" but no matter what it
changes every night
No matter what happened that day my mind still
wants to shut off and just not stay.
Not stay here with all these terrible thoughts no
matter what I do they just won't fuck off
I'm sorry I'm lying
I just don't want to keep trying
I don't want to join the fight
So please life just take me tonight

Before You Go To Bed At Night

Before you go to bed at night
Before you turn off the light
Do you ever just lay there and ask yourself am I
really alright?
Or is every single day just a fight.
A fight to find happiness
A fight to find meaning
A fight to keep going and keep yourself from
bleeding
What am I missing? What can't I see? Why does
everyone I know seem to be happy unlike me?
In our beginning is in fact our end, yet we live
our lives almost as if it were pretend
Maybe life is all a dream and none of this is real,
but each day I wake up I know I'll have to deal
With the thoughts that plague my mind that
think I shouldn't have to feel,
I shouldn't have to feel this way, I shouldn't want
to die, each night I lay in bed and still ask the
sky why.
Why am I here? Why is anyone alive? If in our
beginning is our end why even try?
With no answer, no sign of light
I finally put my head down and say goodnight.

I hope I wake up and this is all a dream, but like
everything in life nothing is what it seems. the
sun rises and I'm still here,
but how long can one go on hoping the end is
near?

Someday

I think about it everyday and all you can say is it
will get better someday.
I'm tired of waiting for some day as some day
never comes
if it was a day of the week than the deal would
be done.
I think about it
everyday
and all you can say is
It will get better
someday
I dream of life up in the clouds and my heart at
peace.
Even if leaving loved ones behind
forever missing a piece.
I think about it
everyday
and all you can say is it will get better
someday
I'm trying to keep fighting each and
everyday,
sometimes I fail and for now that's ok,
I just got to keep on believing there is a
"someday"

Win or Lose

What if I said I just can't do it anymore
I know I've said it before

I can't keep pretending that I want to stay
When all I can think about lately is how I can
end it one day

I have done so much work to find peace in my
heart
I went back to the start

I know what has happened to me has shaped me
into who I am today
And I wouldn't be "me" if it didn't go this way

I felt like I've done everything to see the light
Once again I'm getting tired of the fight

Call me lazy, ungrateful, just a miserable fuck
But I'm sorry I don't see how being born is a
stroke of luck

I don't want to have a house to try and maintain,
more days than not it drives me insane

If something's wrong I want someone to come
save me
I'm sorry, mom and dad, but this is how it be

I'm tired of trying to figure out what to eat,
how to plan for the future,
what to do with my time
See what happens?
All I do is try and rhyme

I don't know as much as I should at thirty-three
And you know what?
That's pretty scary when I know
One day you both won't be able to be here with
me

I don't wanna be Kelsey's problem one day
I've took enough time and attention away

I don't want the girls to have to come and visit
their fucked up aunt in providence care
That's something that I wouldn't want for them,
it's just not fair

I don't get why dying by suicide
is such a big deal
If I died from cancer, or a accident
your heart would have a different feel

I believe suicide is just a cause of death like any
other disease
Can you see my reasoning for believing this,
please?

I feel as if I have a kind of brain brain cancer
and
there is no cure
Until our last breath I guess
we are never sure

I am the master of my fate
and I have the right to choose
If I win the race or ultimately
lose

What The Water Gave Me

I don't think the fantasy is ever going to
disappear
You know the one I always talk about, the one
that makes you all upset to hear

There's a song that sometimes I'll play on repeat
The lyrics make me tap my feet

The song is called funeral and I guess the title
kinda gives the theme away
Kinda just like this poems first line does in that
way

"And last night I blacked out in my car
And I woke up in my childhood bed
Wishin' I was someone else, feelin' sorry for
myself
When I remembered someone's kid is dead"

I've always had a fantasy in my head and can
visualize it clear as day
Pedal to the floor, driving the rocket down
County Road 6,
Stairway To Heaven playing
and my final thoughts just fading away

Anytime I hear that someone has gone into the
water
and it seems to maybe be planned
I can't help but say
"Damn"
Why did I just try that, "that" day?

"And I have this dream where I'm screamin'
underwater
While my friends are wavin' from the shore
And I don't need you to tell me what that means
I don't believe in that stuff anymore"

I believe the fantasy came true just in a different
way
I'm so drawn and connected to the water
it kept calling me
I just had to keep listening for what it had to say

"I am here to cool your body, help it become
more strong and healthy and connect you with
people that will love and understand you, Jenna I
will never drown you."

I don't think the fantasy is ever going to
disappear

You know the one I always talk about now
The one where I am in the water safe
Surrounded by others chanting
"And she's buying the Stairway To Heaven….."

I Asked Alice

The first gift he ever gave me ended up being
the last
It was like this keychain somehow knew our
relationships forecast

As always he chose what we view
It didn't matter if it was dose day, my birthday,
just to name two

He chose that Dose Day that we should watch
both Alice in Wonderland and Through the
looking glass too
I just thought to myself - Hey!
There's no point in voicing any other opinion so
just agree and do

Before I continue I must admit although I am
almost 35 maybe to much surprise
I am not much familiarized with Wonderland
I have heard parts before, I know about the
rabbit hole and a talking cat
but not much more than that

I was feeling pretty good enjoying myself taking
in all the visuals, intense colour and sound

When something disgusting, wet, I feel fell on
my feet planted warmly on the ground

He had vomited up the mushrooms and was
unable to trip
But here I was left feeling good, trying to take in
the movie
and now I have to babysit

I was glad when the night was over and was able
to go to bed
I didn't have much to say that night
I felt everything had been said

I woke up that morning to him playing a
upsetting podcast
that he knew would hurt my heart
I asked him what was going on
He said nothing
Upstairs I went to to start...

To start to cry and scream at myself
Why did you do this again to your family Jenna
again to yourself?
You have two choices
Wait till November and attempt once more
and put it on him - even the score
Or grab your Cat and your Bong
And go home to your parents and accept defeat

Only then once again can we rise to our feet

So 72 hours later I grabbed my bong and my cat
and since then the real, true, honest, authentic
Alice has not once looked back

Alice found her way out of the rabbit hole and
you can too
It's incredible what setting an intention can truly
do

The first gift he ever gave me ended up being
the last one
When I look at this keychain all I see is
a problem 'shrooms helped me figure out
That's it, Done

The secret, Alice, is to surround yourself with
people who
make your heart smile. It's then, only then, that
you'll find
Wonderland.

The Smell of Polo

It still feels like yesterday
25 years still doesn't take the pain away
The pain of all the things you couldn't be here
for
The pain of never seeing you once more
I can't remember how your voice sounded when
you spoke
or when you told a funny joke
I look at a few pictures of you everyday, the one
of you kissing La on her cheek
It always reminds me of the love I always seek
When I'm at your house where you lived for
many years
Things can still bring me to tears
When I go to the bathroom i always go in the
medicine cabinet,
it's has long ago become a habit
I always smell the Polo, take a deep breath and
try not to feel sorrow
You are still here with us in some way
Someway, somehow you are mentioned or
thought of everyday
I love being with La and hearing all the tales, in
the end it all means love never really fails

I don't believe in god or really a higher power
but deep inside I believe you were there that
hour
I believe you saved me that night I tried to
finally be with you
You said "Jenna your life is not yet through"
It still feels like yesterday
25 years doesn't take the pain away
The pain of all you couldn't be here for
Oh if I could only see you once more

February 20, 2020

Cuz I'm Your Dad

It's Father's Day today
and I'm blessed to say for me it's not just
another day

You have been in my life from the very
beginning and continue to be a big part of the
reason I'm still here and breathing

You had already became a father when you
found out I was on the way
We are one family
It's still something I know I thank you for till
this day

When Mommy worked weekends we hung out
with you
While you had a nap we found things to do
We'd play Barbies and wander with kids down
the street
But boy were we scared when we heard those
boot covered feet!

As I got older our relationship grew in a new
way
I think it was partly age and maturity

being able for us both to express better what we
say

Our Daddy/Jenna days are always something to
remember and laugh about
Cuz something usually goes a little wrong
without a doubt

We enjoy going for a nice drive and stopping
along the way
One of my favourites is to sit at the water, take
in the day
and of course a stop a Circle K

Dad I know I have hurt you many times over the
years
and though you shed few, I know I've caused
you tears

You've been the Dad I've needed since my first
breath
I'm forever sorry for trying to control my death

Thank you for loving the daughter you got,
I know although I question sometimes
I know you don't give it another thought

"I love you Jenna every single day whether the
day is good, bad or sad"

"But why?"
"It's cuz I'm your Dad"

"I am your father, I am not your friend
I'm here to help guide you though life until my
life's end"

I often look at one of the very first pictures of
you and me
and you holding me in your arms as I sleep
Even now when my heart is broken
I still run into your arms and you hold me as I
weep

I continue to learn from you each and everyday,
whether it's asking for an opinion, advice,
or just how to use the sander the right way

Thank you for always being a father
I can be proud of to say is mine
I'm really looking forward
to us having more time

More time for adventures
to places we like to be
and some that we
have yet to see

You are the best Father for me in every way,
even if you can't really cook that well...
I'm grateful for you everyday

The Mother I Need

This is a poem for you
I know it's way overdue
But today is a special day
It's Mother's Day

Everyday is special
that is spent with you
I always enjoy when
it is just us two

We can be shopping, or walking, cooking or
cleaning.
but even though these things can sometimes feel
like chores
with you there it always feels like meaning

You have always been there for me on happy
days and sad
and for that I am always glad

I'm sorry I have broke your heart so many times
and could have left you guessing forever
"How did I miss the signs?"

Mom, I wouldn't be here if it wasn't for you

you make me want to keep fighting with all that
do

I'm forever sorry I tried to take the life you gave
it's a weight in my heart that I will carry to my
grave

You're the mother I needed when I was three
and having seizures in the night
I think it was as early as then that
We knew for life I'd have to fight.

You're the mother I needed when I was
struggling in school,
you always made me, not feel like a fool

You're the mother I needed when I was first
taken advantage of
I will always remember when I told you with
Leonard
and your amazing love

You're the mother I needed and still do to help
me know left from right,
it always amazes me you can usually tell where I
am
from just what I say is in sight

You're the mother I needed when my body was
pregnant but I wanted to be not.
I told you my wishes and I don't think you gave
it another thought.
You stayed in the room with me and held my
hand as we both cried.
This moment thank you again
Thank you again for being at my side.

You're the mother I needed to have to help get
me though school, honestly my diploma should
be a "Duo"

You're the mother I needed when I told you it
happened again, that I said "I need to smoke
weed, or this could be the end"

"Jenna I'm so sorry the world keeps hurting you
please know it has nothing to do with you
you are strong and brave, loving and kind
and when I look at you
I'm always glad your mine"

You're the best mother one could ever be blessed
with
always know your life is a gift

You're the mother I needed and still need
everyday

There could be a million things more I could say

I think I'll end it with "thank you for always
making me feel, some type of way"

Still a Loose Girl

Four years ago today I said yes
to a relationship I knew, deep down, was
doomed from the start
When you take the guy to a court house to pay
abuse charges on the second date
you should know he's prolly gonna hurt your
heart

Last night I got a message from a guy I've been
seeing casually for awhile
Usually it would begin with a hello or at least a
smile
We haven't spoken for a few weeks and I kinda
thought we were just kinda done
So when a message popped up my mind kinda
spun

All he sent was a peach and a wave
Luckily I was right on my phone so I could click
and save
All this means is a ass slap - that is all
Even after this amount of time fuck you think
you would even call

Four years and it feels like it's still the same

Am I the one who is to blame?

I always get used for my body, that's what they
like best,
or once they get it they lay it to rest

I'm done searching for the one
if there is one for me
What I've been doing, hasn't been working, the
last decade
plus we can very well see

Whatever my love story is - if there is one
will be up to destiny.

You Are The Same As You Ever Was

Hey it's your Blue Jay
I talk to you almost everyday
But today is a day I have some things to say
and turns out it's your birthday

You enjoy Peace signs, flowers, music, cats and
the little joys of the day
Like sitting by a fire, lighting one up and just
taking in the day
All the while hearing the music play

You've always been our cool
Aunt Sherrie
It's probably the biggest memories I carry
You always let Kels and I touch and play with
whatever we wanted,
it was our say
As a aunt myself, I've come a long way but this
is something I need to work on
till this day

Thank you for all the experiences you've shared
It really shows how much you've cared

I'll always remember going to concerts with you
I really hope that that's something, someday we
can still do

Us going to see B.N.L
It's always a story I want to tell
It's memories like this that I won't ever forget
I can't believe Jim Creegan and I actually met

"If I had a million dollars" there would be some
things
 we would have to do,
one of them is, for sure,
is getting another auntie/niece matching tattoo

I am so grateful for how close we've gotten as
the years have gone by
I will forever be sorry for trying to control when
I say goodbye

I love being able to share whatever is on my
mind,
nothings off the table and no matter what your
always kind

You never "bite me" or "twist my arm"
You are really not one to cause harm

You tell me "All you gotta do is send for me",
"Don't wait too long" , "Just pick up the phone
and I'll be there, where I belong"
Thank you for being a huge reason I love song

"But let me get to the point, let's roll another
joint
And turn the radio loud"

Don't You Want To See How It Ends?

Don't you want to see how it ends?
The end of of it all
The final curtain call

I always want to hear a song till the very end
Close my eyes and play the days I'm glad I
stayed over in my head

Do I want to stay and see how it ends for me
By not my own hands, by fate, just wait and see

No dress rehearsal this is our life I have tattooed
on my arm
it's there for a purpose just not something to
cover surface

It's a reminder to me that this is my life and this
journey is mine,
and it would be unfair to end it before it's truly
my time

So yes I want to stay and see how it ends
The end of it all
The final curtain call
Where I will stand proudly and take my final
bow